Copyright & Terms of Use

About Lela Stankovic

"The higher your structure is to be, the deeper must be its foundation." - Saint Augustine

Lela has always admired the great artists of past centuries like Vermeer, Titian and Rembrandt who have gifted us those timeless treasures that transcend the boundaries of time and geography.

Inspired by the Great Masters, firmly grounded in studio practice and yet pursuing cross-disciplinary inquiry, Lela continually seeks to discover new ways to give form to her voice. Lela's art seeks to integrate the techniques of Old Masters with the inspirations from today's world.

Acquired by art collectors in US, Canada and in Europe, Lela's paintings adorn private homes as well as offices and commercial establishments.

Lela loves to explore new elements in her Oil & Watercolor paintings and her paintings and drawings reflect the joy to be had in simple things, the exuberance of the flowers, a honey bee sucking nectar, or simply, the magic of everyday life.

www.lelacreations.com

Introduction

It was July 1st, and a large charity event celebrating Canada Day brought to my attention the most beautiful cupcakes I have ever seen. Some of them were simple, colored in Canada flag red and white colors, and then others were very exotict and really breathtaking. For me as an artist, I did not feel like eating them. I felt I should just frame them in the picture and leave there to marvel forever.

And that is where the idea to create a coloring book capturing these magnificent creations was born.

I wanted to capture their beauty for all of you to enjoy, relax and learn and advance as an artist while coloring their intricate shapes and details.

Many people who would like to start painting ask me what they should paint to start with, and then what should be next. Very often new aspiring artists face a roadblock of not knowing what to paint. We all know that fear of blank page. Even more importantly how complex should their first subject be, and how to progressively advance and increase complexity of the chosen subjects without feeling overwhelmed.

What is inside this book?

This book contains 8 cupcake designs to color. Each of them is printed in 3 different shades of gray to the total of 24 coloring pages. The first one has completely black outline, the second has middle gray outline, and the third has a very light gray outline. The benefit of having various gray scale outlines is to allow you to practice various coloring techniques and see which effect you like the most. A page with a black outline will give the appearance of a line and wash painting. The middle gray and light gray will support a painting where you do not want to have a very pronounced outline, and would like to allow the vibrancy of the color to shine through without an interference of the outline.

It will guide you on your artistic journey from a very simple Canada maple leaf cupcake design, through slowly increasing complexity and more advanced additional 7 designs. You will be advancing from a simple line outline towards more shaded and realistic cupcakes, that once colored will look like as if you can pick them from the page and eat.

What are unique benefits of using a hand drawn coloring book like this one?

The first benefit is a natural and realistic appearance of the drawing, which will guide you through the coloring process making it more relaxing and enjoyable. All drawings in this book are hand drawn on a paper, and scanned, and hand shaded with dip pan in black ink. I really wanted to have a variety of shapes and lines which dip pan can create, and offer an artistic and more realistic appearance for you to enjoy.

Second benefit is added shading, which is a great advantage for all of you who would like a small help when deciding which areas should be colored with darker color and which should stay light. That way you will be able to preserve the form of the subject and visually communicate realism. This also builds your observation skills, and be able to see as an artist the world around you. This is a great advantage

Third, I want you to feel a sense of accomplishment with each completed drawing and painting, and proudly move to the next one, sharpening your observation skills and polishing your technical aspects of handling the chosen coloring medium.

What is the best way to use this book?

The pages in this book can be used individually, or as a gift and great fun for your team building or party events.

If you purchased an electronic eBook, you will need to first print the pages on the paper of your choice. This option gives a great flexibility in choosing the best paper for your chosen coloring medium. In general any uncoated, lightly sized drawing paper of 200gsm thickness or less is ideal. It can be printed on a regular home laser or inkjet printer, and used for dry media and light watercolor washes.

Note: In order to print from eBook (Kindle or ePub edition of the book), you will need to "screen capture" the image on your Kindle, Ipad, phone or computer device first, and then print the captured image.

If the copy you purchased is a printed edition, the choice of the paper it was printed on was limited by availability offered from the Amazon printing service.

Let's stay in touch

For further learning, free resources, and guided step by step video tutorials how to color included pages and much more, please join to our www.PaintAndDrawTogether.com artist community, and associated YouTube channel. Share your work and progress. We would like to stay in touch and hear from you.

Other books by Lela

Painting Glorious Rose Flower in Watercolor - in 7 Stages, available on Amazon Kindle, and Apple iBook.

Coloring Pages

There are 8 cupcake designs included. Each is printed in 3 different shades of gray - black, middle, and light gray, suitable for a broader choice of coloring mediums and desired appearance.

Design 1: Maple leaf cupcake
Design 2: St. Valentine heart cupcake
Design 3: Bucket of roses cupcake
Design 4: Sunflower cupcake
Design 5: Bluebery cupcake
Design 6: Strawbery cupcake
Design 7: Easter egg nest cupcake
Design 8: Unicorn cupcake

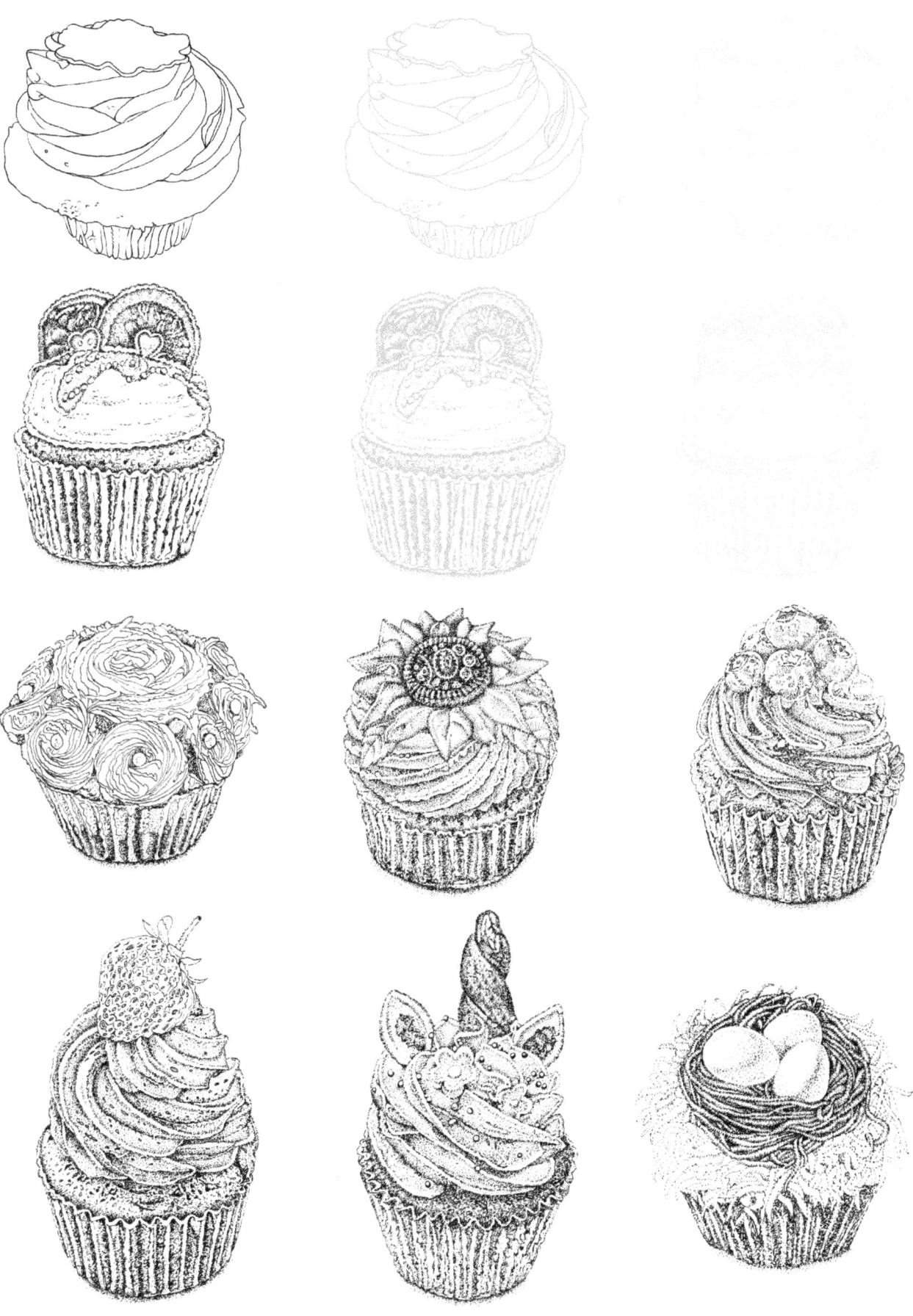

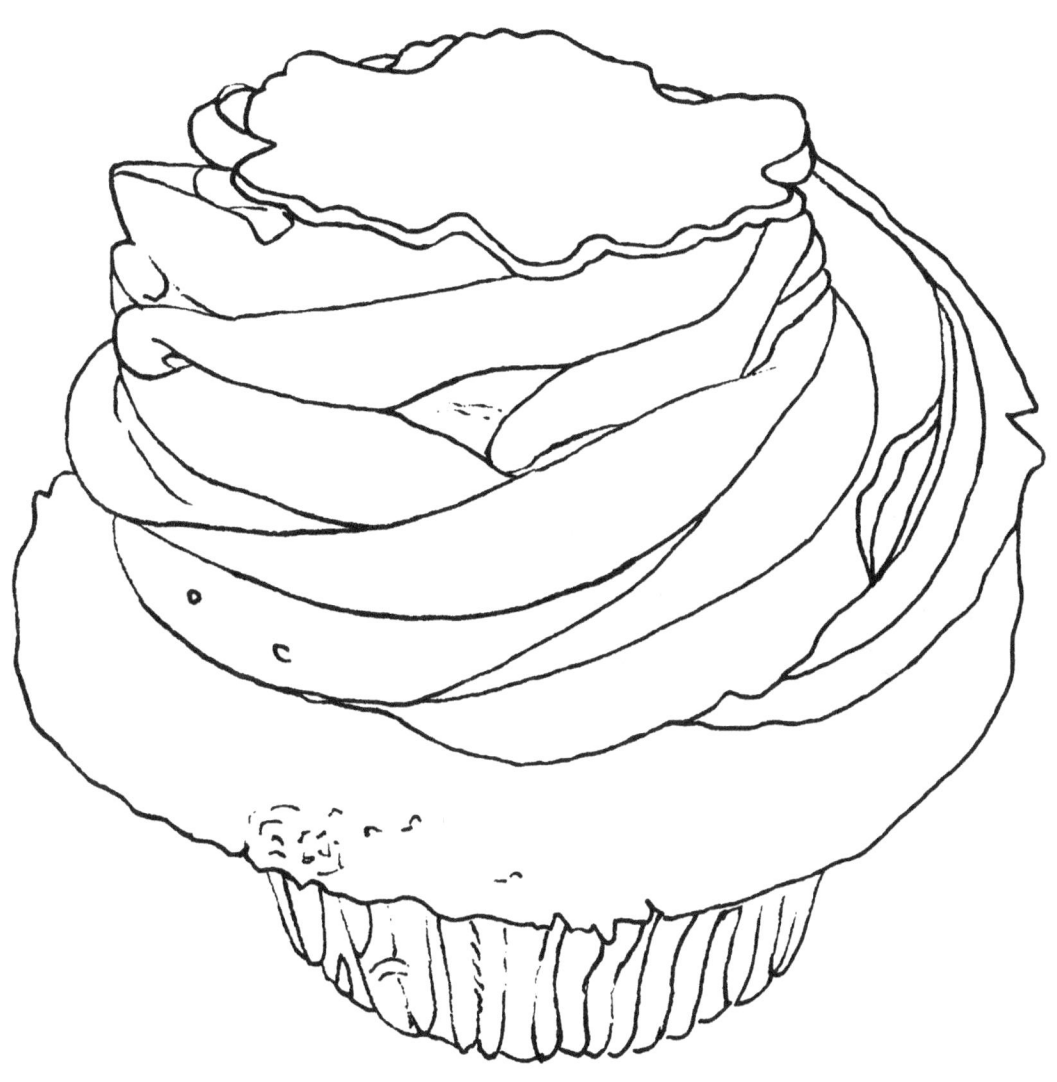

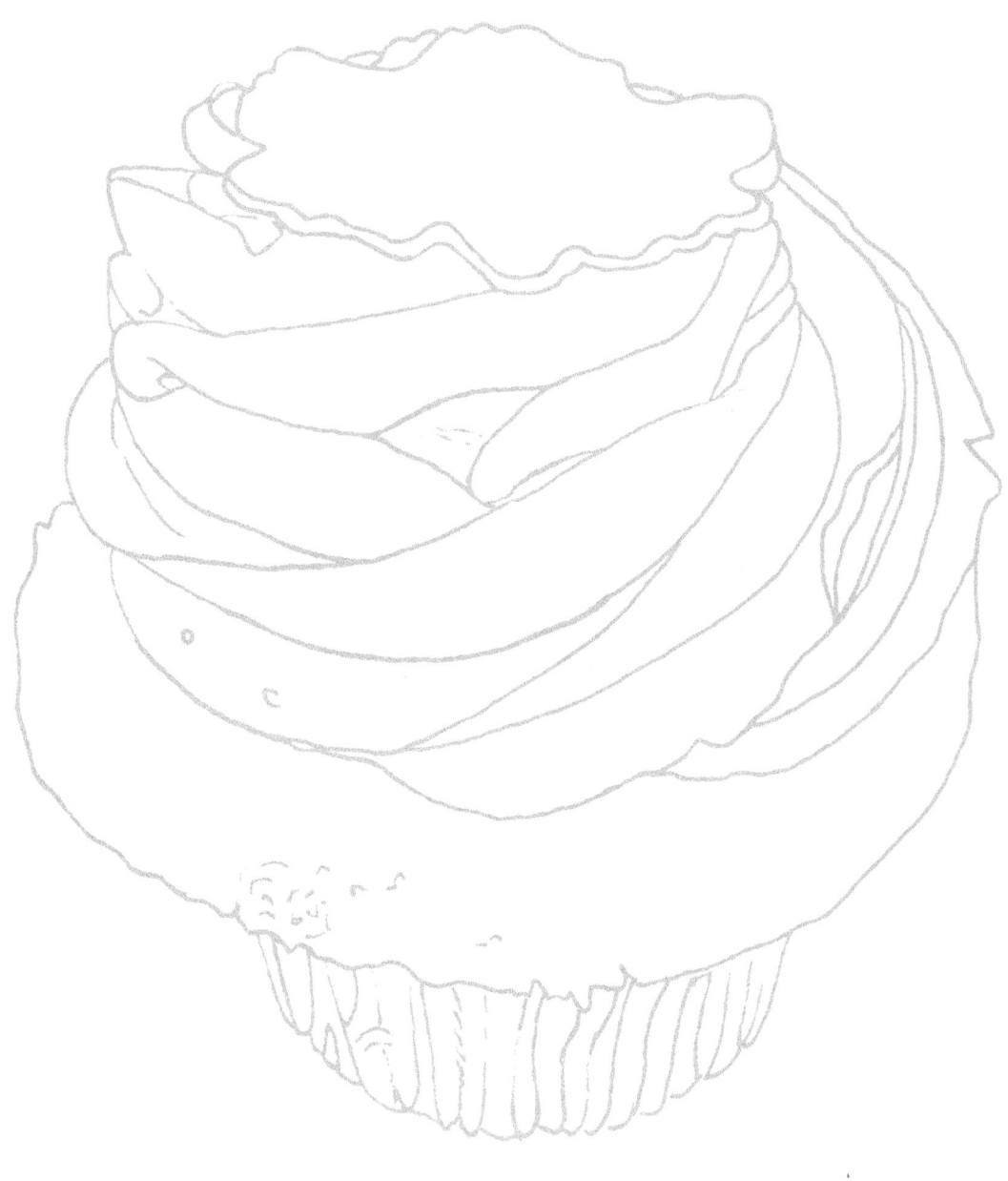

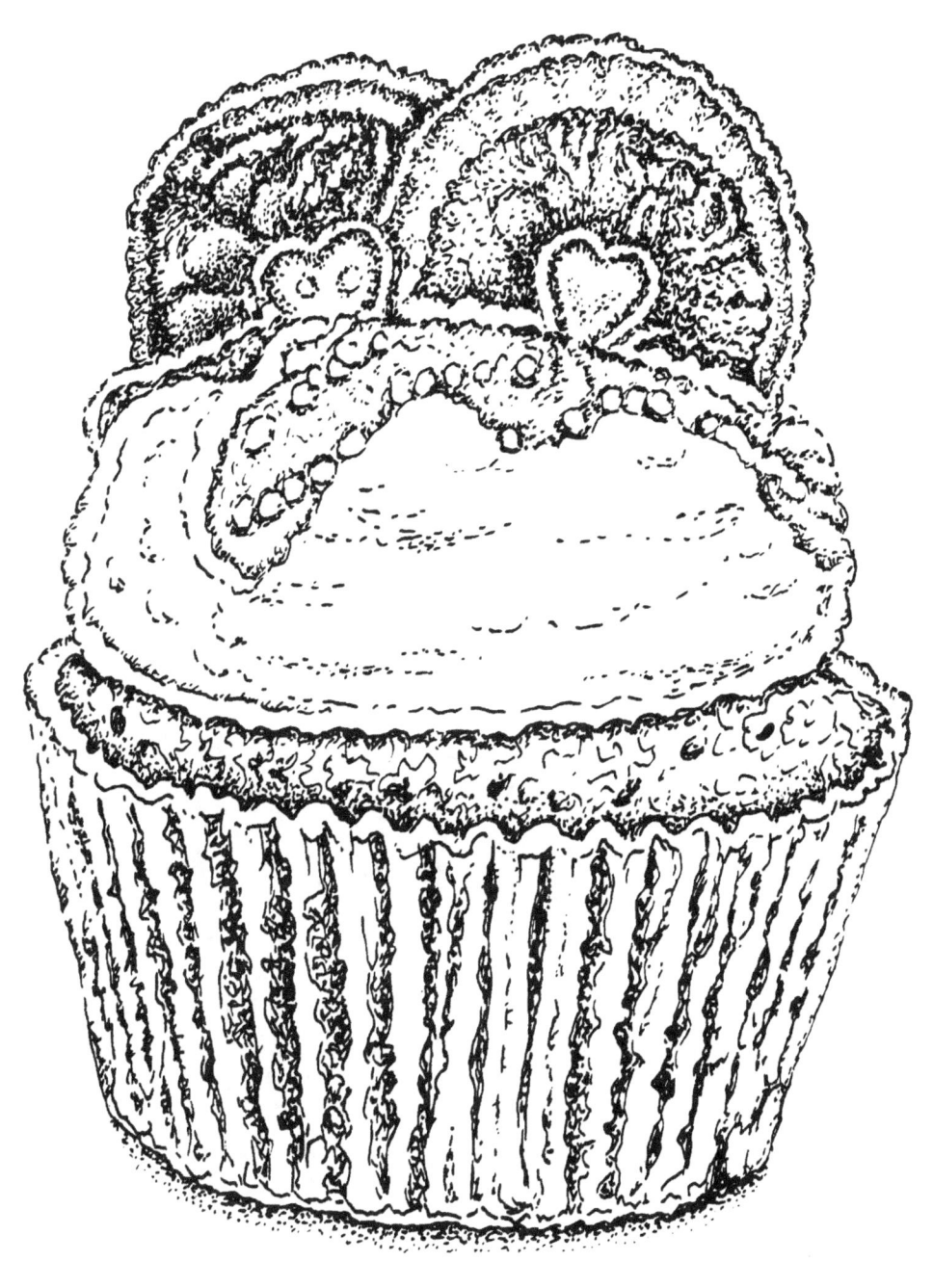

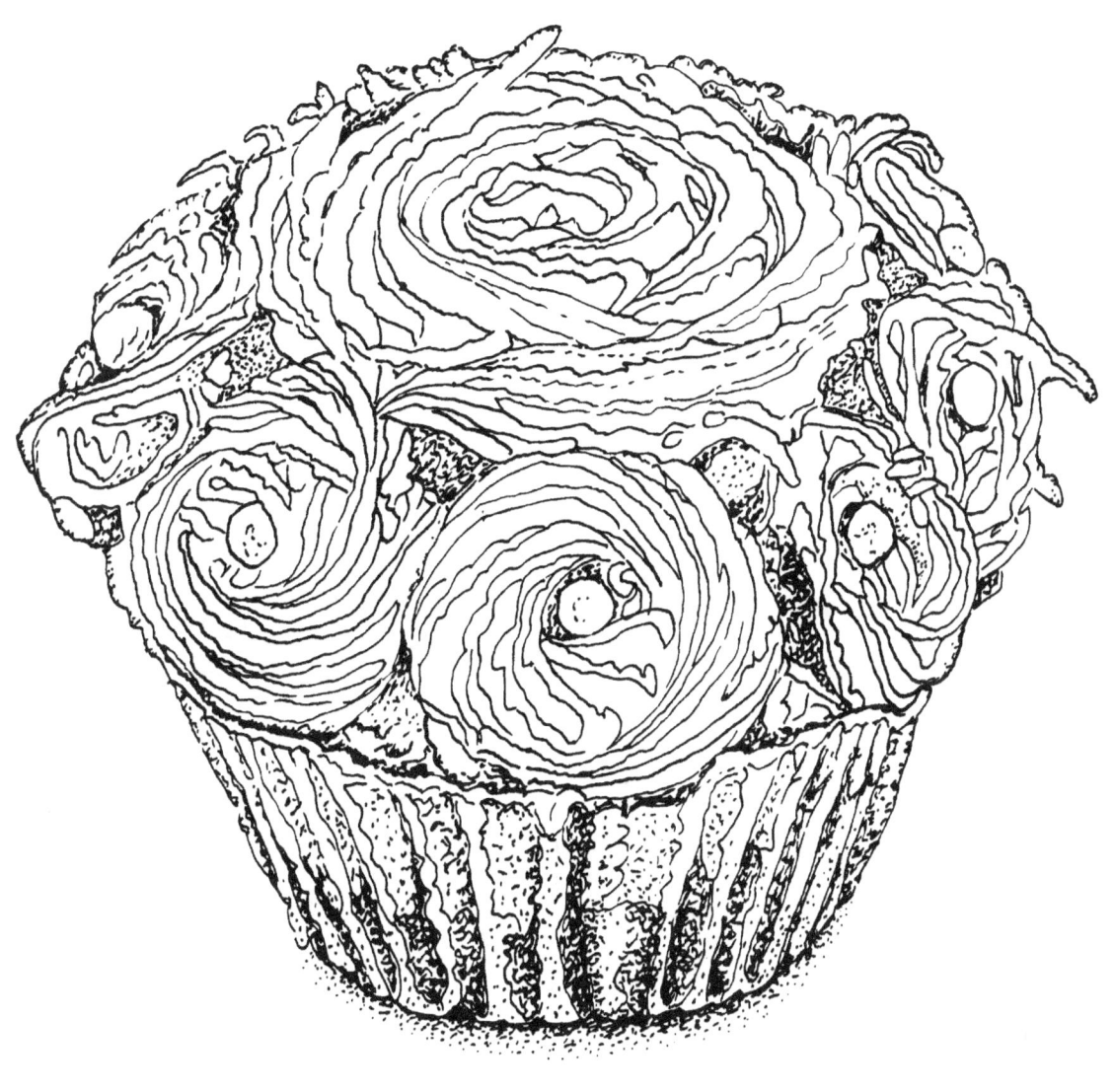

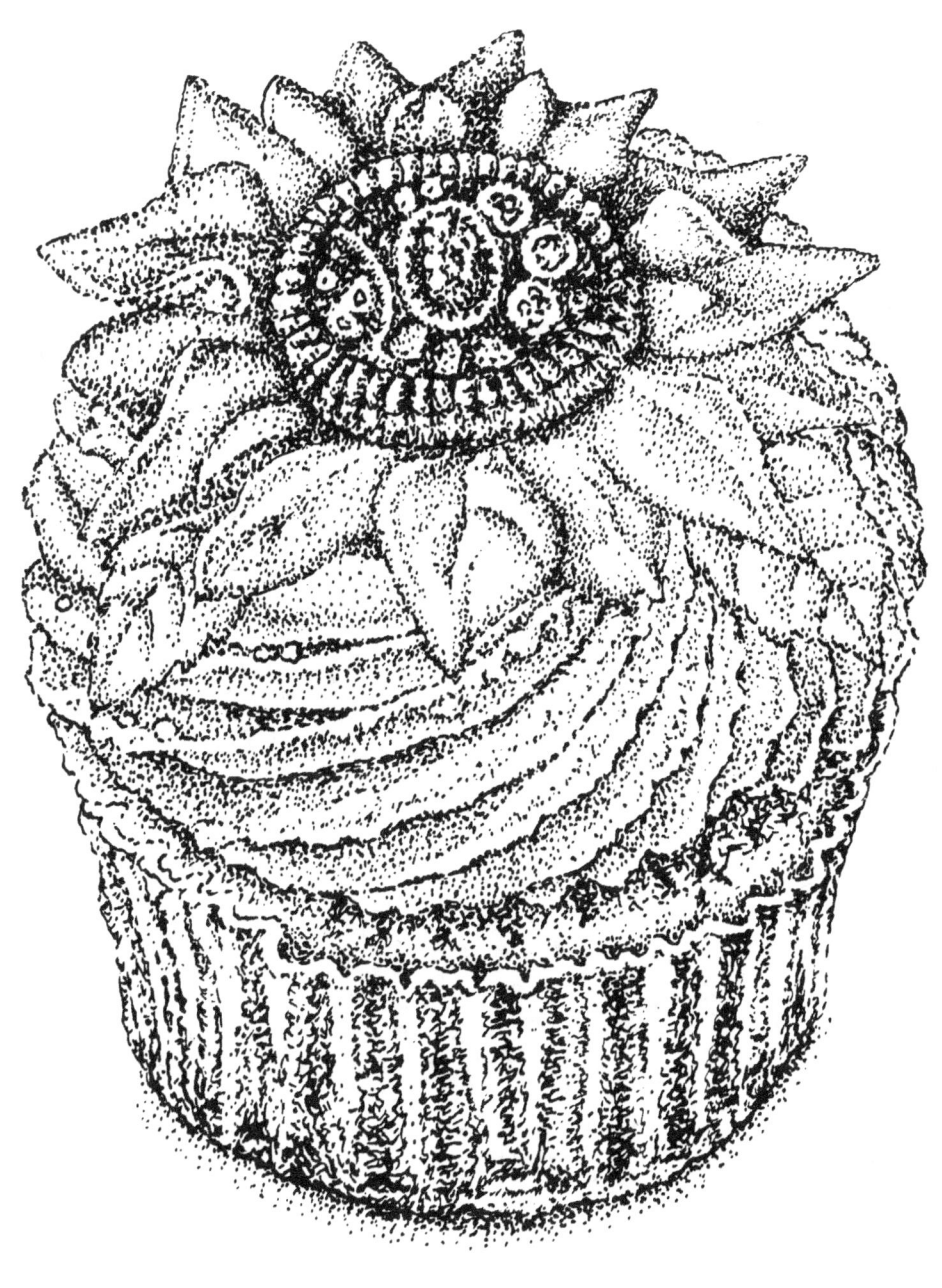

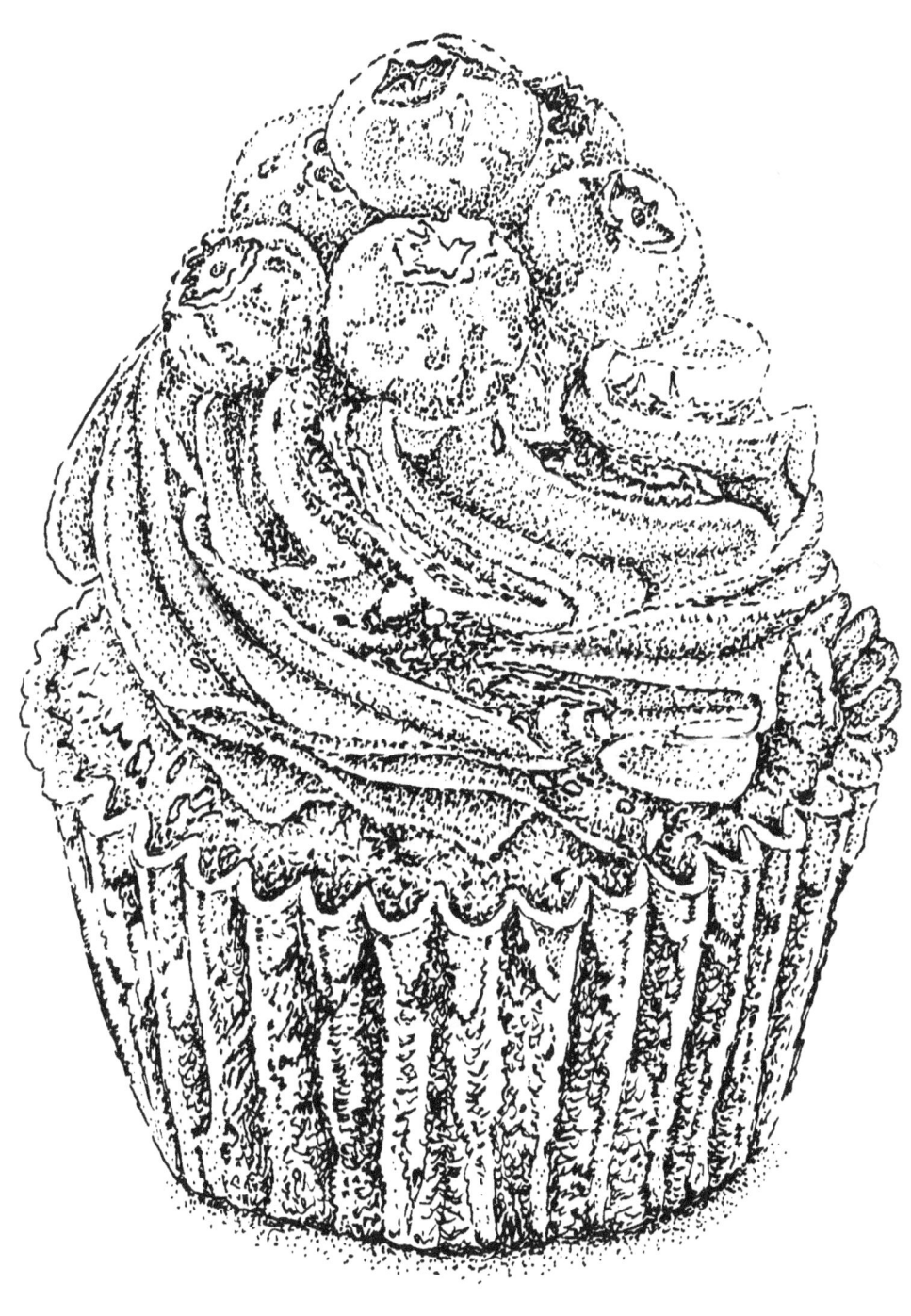

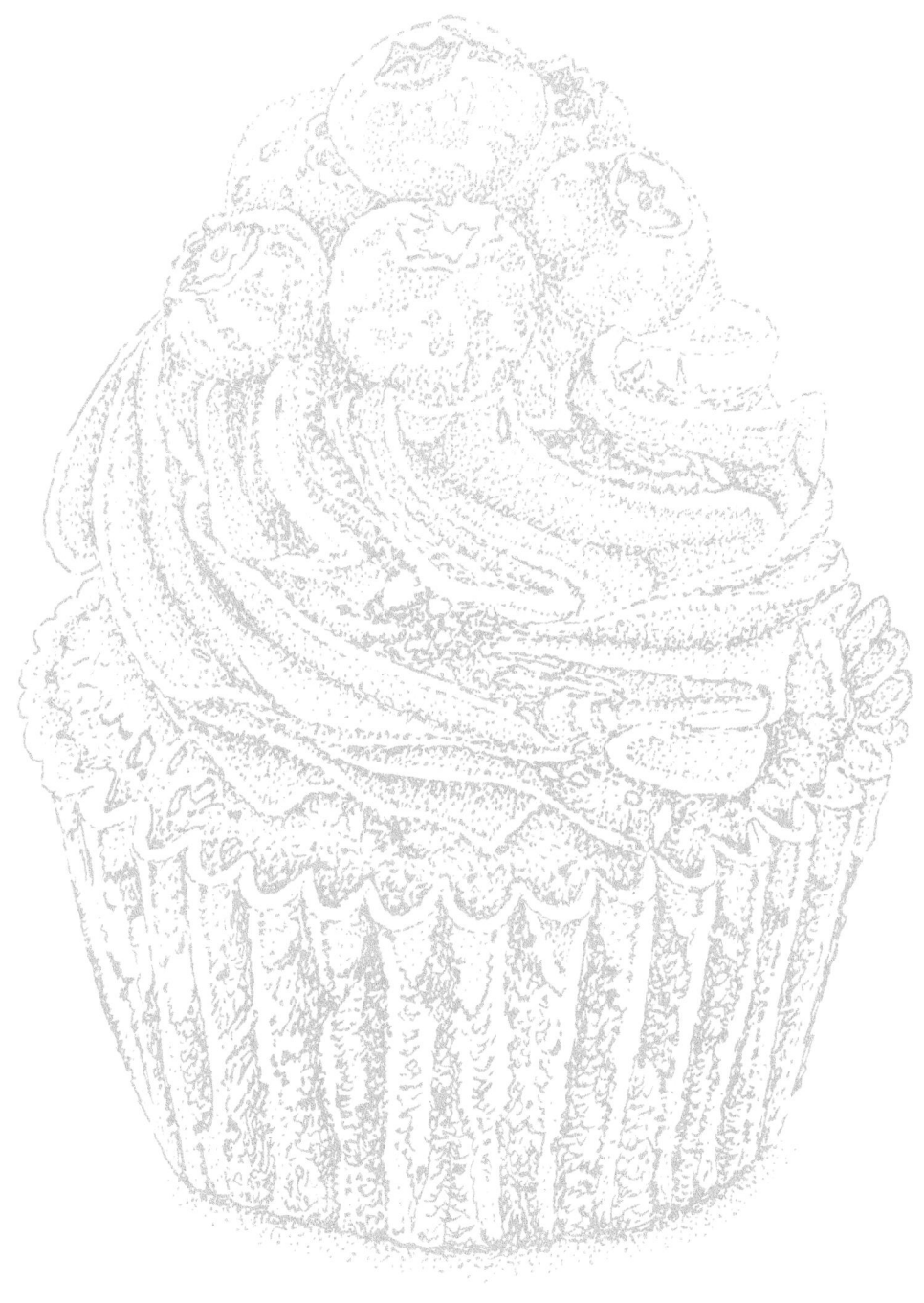

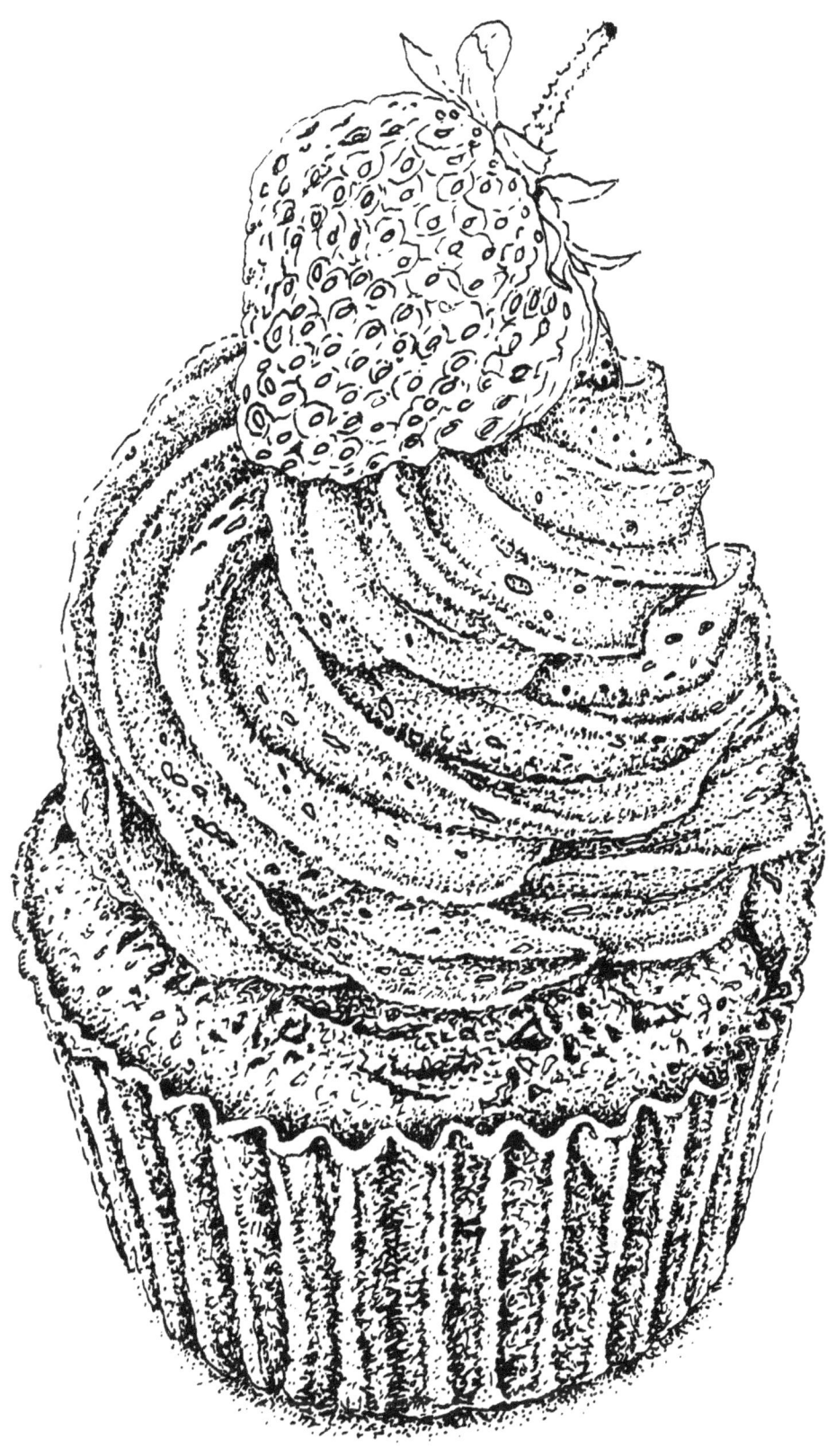

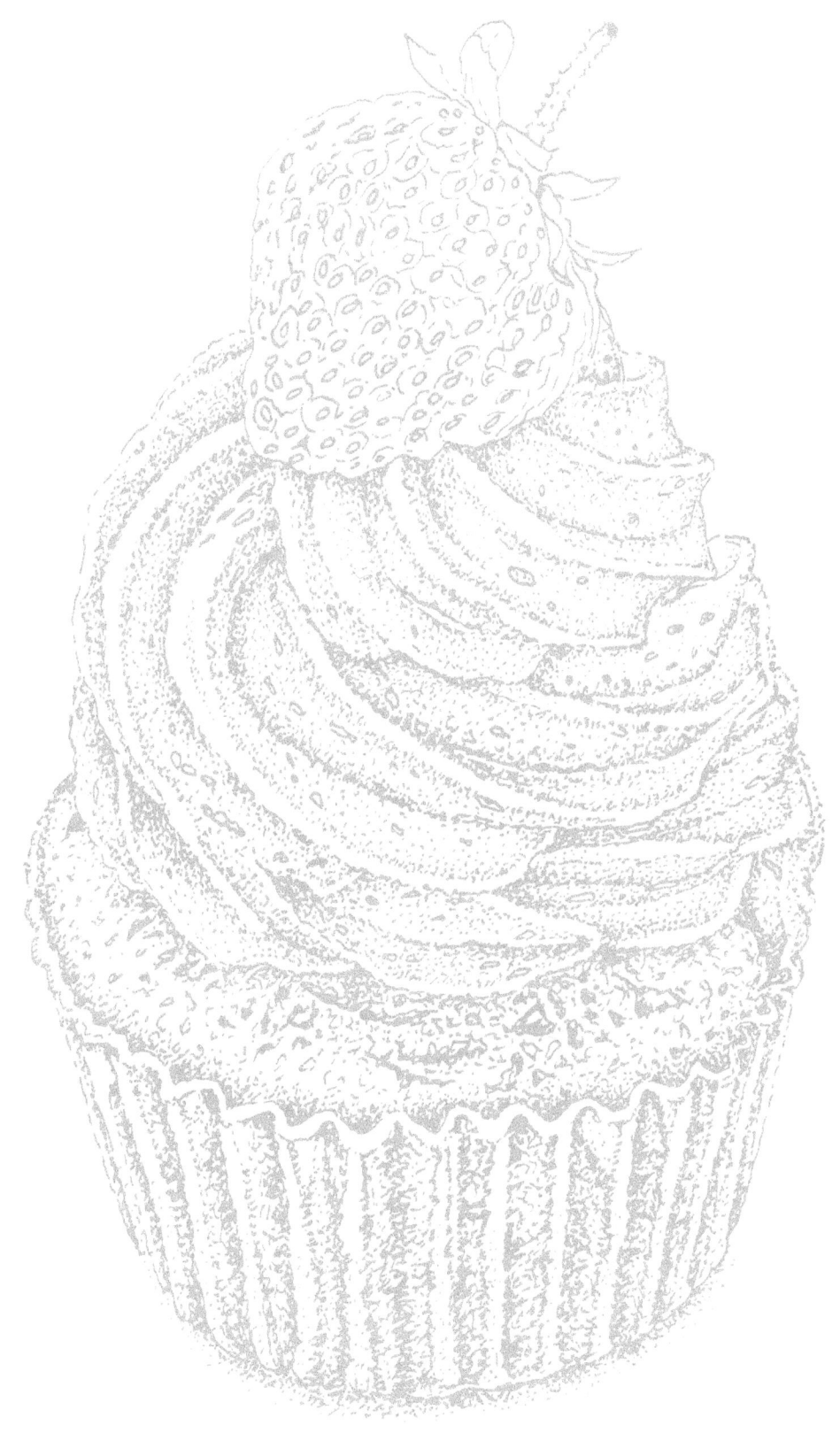

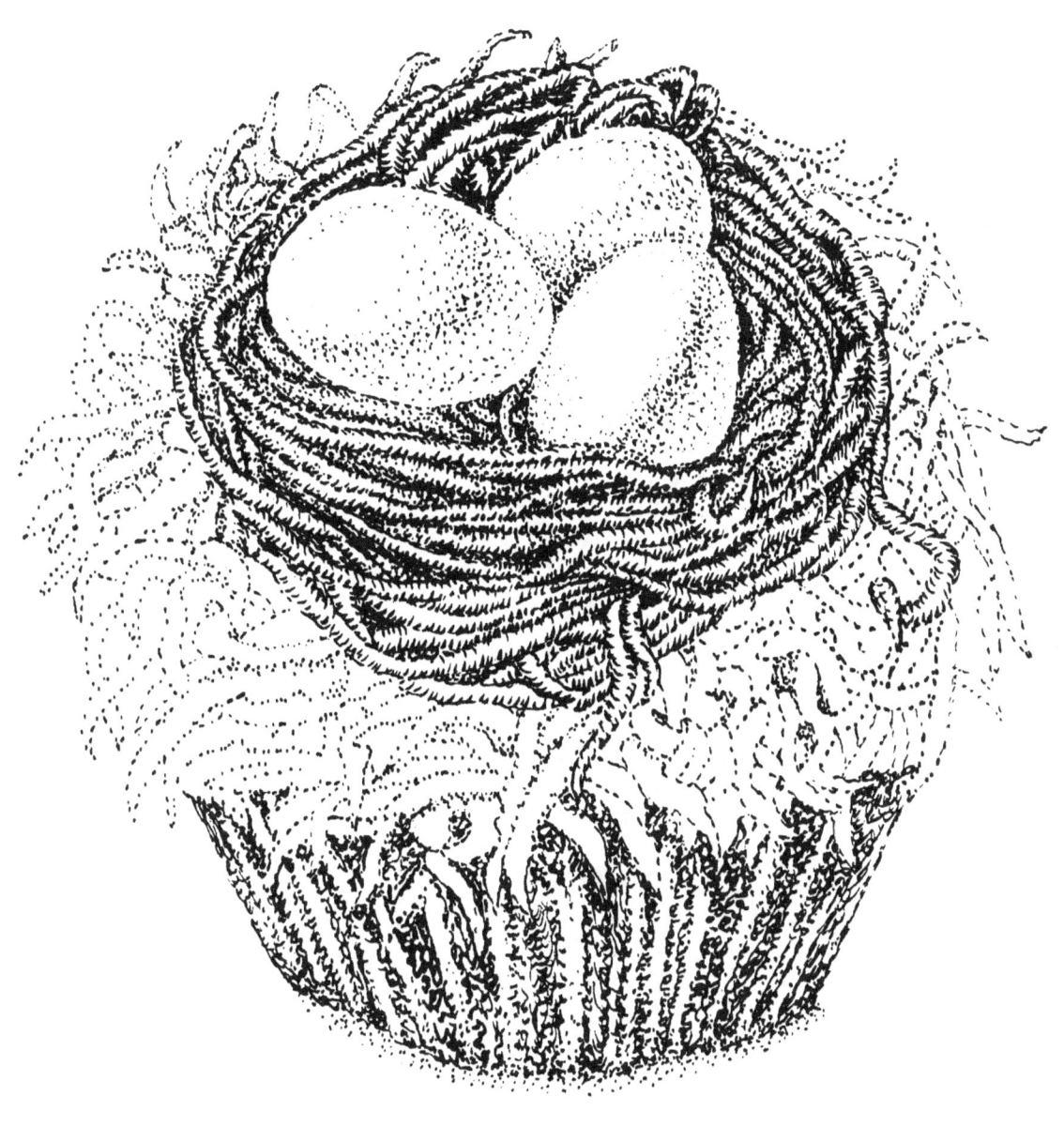

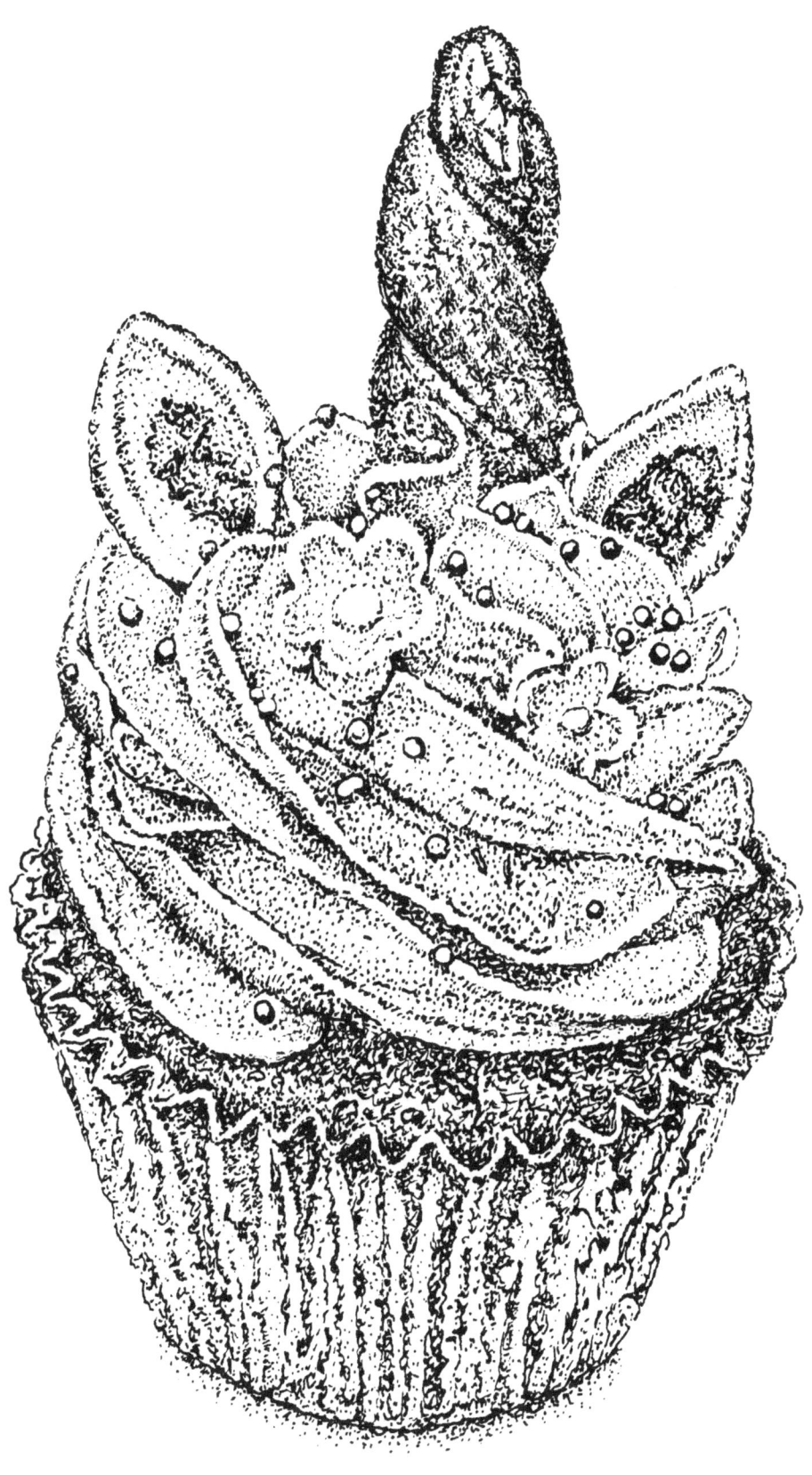

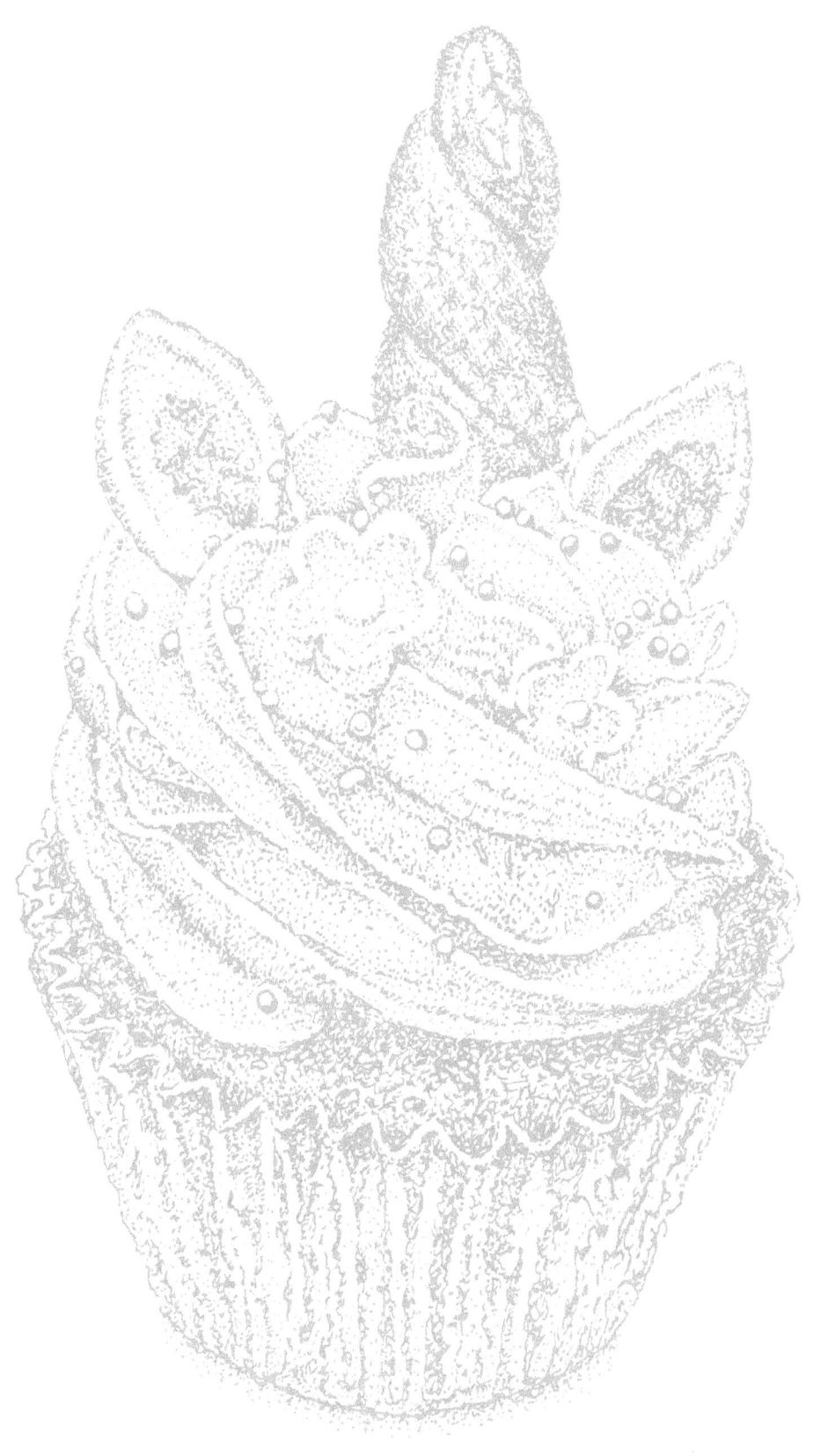

Free Bonus Resources

Please visit and join to **www.PaintAndDrawTogether.com** a free comunity for artists and art lovers.

These free resources are not mandatory requirement to be able to follow this book. They are provided simply as a free bonus to learn and expand further your artistic skills.